Expansion and Reform (Early
1800s-1861)
Daniel Casciato
AR B.L.: 7.2
Points: 2.0

Expansion and Reform
(Early 1800s-1861)

★★ PRESIDENTS OF THE UNITED STATES ★★

By Daniel Casciato

WEIGL PUBLISHERS INC.

Published by Weigl Publishers Inc.
350 5th Avenue, Suite 3304 PMB 6G
New York, NY 10118-0069
Website: www.weigl.com

Library of Congress Cataloging-in-Publication Data

Casciato, Daniel.
  Expansion and reform / Daniel Casciato.
      p. cm. -- (Presidents of the United States)
  Includes bibliographical references and index.
  ISBN 978-1-59036-741-4 (hard cover : alk. paper) -- ISBN 978-1-59036-742-1 (soft cover : alk. paper)
  1. Presidents--United States--History--19th century--Juvenile literature. 2. United States--History--1815-1861--Juvenile literature. 3. United States--Territorial expansion--History--19th century--Juvenile literature. 4. United States--Politics and government--1815-1861--Juvenile literature. I. Title.
  E176.1.C262 2008
  973.5092'2--dc22
  [B]
                                        2007012644

Printed in the United States of America
1 2 3 4 5 6 7 8 9 0 11 10 09 08 07

Project Coordinator
Heather C. Hudak

Design
Terry Paulhus

Photo Credits
Every reasonable effort has been made to trace ownership and to obtain permission to reprint copyright material. The publishers would be pleased to have any errors or omissions brought to their attention so that they may be corrected in subsequent printings.

All of the Internet URLs given in the book were valid at the time of publication. However, due to the dynamic nature of the Internet, some addresses may have changed, or sites may have ceased to exist since publication. While the author and publisher regret any inconvenience this may cause readers, no responsibility for any such changes can be accepted by either the author or the publisher.

Contents

United States Presidents

REVOLUTION AND THE NEW NATION (1750–EARLY 1800s)

 George Washington
(1789–1797)

 John Adams
(1797–1801)

 Thomas Jefferson
(1801–1809)

 James Madison
(1809–1817)

 James Monroe
(1817–1825)

EXPANSION AND REFORM (EARLY 1800s–1861)

 John Quincy Adams
(1825–1829)

 Andrew Jackson
(1829–1837)

 Martin Van Buren
(1837–1841)

 William Henry Harrison
(1841)

 John Tyler
(1841–1845)

 James Polk
(1845–1849)

 Zachary Taylor
(1849–1850)

 Millard Fillmore
(1850–1853)

 Franklin Pierce
(1853–1857)

 James Buchanan
(1857–1861)

CIVIL WAR AND RECONSTRUCTION (1850–1877)

 Abraham Lincoln
(1861–1865)

 Andrew Johnson
(1865–1869)

 Ulysses S. Grant
(1869–1877)

DEVELOPMENT OF THE INDUSTRIAL UNITED STATES (1870–1900)

 Rutherford B. Hayes
(1877–1881)

 James Garfield
(1881)

 Chester Arthur
(1881–1885)

 Grover Cleveland
(1885–1889)
(1893–1897)

 Benjamin Harrison
(1889–1893)

 William McKinley
(1897–1901)

THE EMERGENCE OF MODERN AMERICA (1890–1930)

 Theodore Roosevelt
(1901–1909)

 William H. Taft
(1909–1913)

 Woodrow Wilson
(1913–1921)

 Warren Harding
(1921–1923)

 Calvin Coolidge
(1923–1929)

THE GREAT DEPRESSION AND WORLD WAR II (1929–1945)

 Herbert Hoover
(1929–1933)

 Franklin D. Roosevelt
(1933–1945)

POST-WAR UNITED STATES (1945–EARLY 1970s)

 Harry S. Truman
(1945–1953)

 Dwight Eisenhower
(1953–1961)

 John F. Kennedy
(1961–1963)

 Lyndon Johnson
(1963–1969)

CONTEMPORARY UNITED STATES (1968 TO THE PRESENT)

 Richard Nixon
(1969–1974)

 Gerald Ford
(1974–1977)

 Jimmy Carter
(1977–1981)

 Ronald Reagan
(1981–1989)

 George H. W. Bush
(1989–1993)

 William J. Clinton
(1993–2001)

 George W. Bush
(2001–)

Expansion and Reform

Throughout the 1800s, the United States would expand its territory either by buying land or acquiring it through war.

"Who, then, can doubt that our country is destined to be the great nation of futurity?"

John L. O'Sullivan, magazine editor

The years from 1801 to 1860 were a period of expansion and reform in the United States. This era began with the presidency of Thomas Jefferson, the author of the Declaration of Independence. In 1803, Jefferson bought a large piece of land from France that stretched from the Mississippi River to the Rocky Mountains. Known as the Louisiana Purchase, it doubled the size of the United States. By the mid-1800s, the United States' borders would reach as far west as the Pacific Ocean.

During this period of U.S. history, the United States needed to prove itself as an independent nation. Even though it had gained freedom from Great Britain in the Revolutionary War, there were many struggles ahead. The British still had a strong influence in the region. European countries, such as Spain and France, owned land in the Americas. Other countries, such as Russia and Mexico, wished to colonize parts of North America.

One of the United States' first tests of independence was the War of 1812. The British prevented U.S. trade overseas and helped American Indians defend land that the United States wished to settle. Americans went to war with the British once again. Fighting for its rights against a powerful nation like Great Britain proved to the world that the United States was a strong, independent nation. Yet, this would not be the only time that the United States would stand up to a world power.

As the nation grew, so did the issues of **states' rights** and slavery. Some people saw an increasing need for slaves as the United States gained territory. They thought slaves were needed to farm the land. **Abolitionists** wanted to end slavery. They viewed the enslavement of other people as wrong and unjust. People often argued whether it was up to state governments or the federal government to decide if slavery should be allowed in new territories.

Politics divided many people. The beginning of the expansion and reform era was known as the Virginia **dynasty**. Three presidents, Thomas Jefferson, James Madison, and James Monroe, were elected between 1800 and 1820. They were all from Virginia and belonged to the Democratic-Republican Party. Members of this party ran against each other in the 1824 presidential election. John Quincy Adams and Andrew Jackson were among the most popular candidates, and neither was from Virginia. The election was highly contested. As a result, the election caused a split in the Democratic-Republican Party. Followers of Adams and Jackson would eventually form separate political parties.

Following the Virginia dynasty, the formation of new political parties would be just one of many struggles faced by U.S. presidents. The Expansion and Reform Era would be filled with wars and economic troubles. Two presidents would die in office, and several issues would threaten to divide the country in two.

John Quincy Adams' Early Years

John Quincy Adams was born on July 11, 1767, in Braintree, Massachusetts. Adams was the oldest son of Abigail and John Adams, the second president of the United States. His father's influence led to Adams involvement in politics at a young age. He would eventually become president, and he would be the first president whose father had served as president.

> **"If your actions inspire others to dream more, learn more, do more and become more, you are a leader."**
>
> *From the diary of John Quincy Adams*

Adams grew up during the Revolutionary War, which began when he was seven years old. He even watched the famous Battle of Bunker Hill from a hilltop near his family's home. During this battle, colonists defended Boston from a large force of British soldiers.

At age ten, Adams traveled with his father on a diplomatic mission to France. He spent much of his childhood overseas and went to school in Europe. Adams learned to speak several languages, including French, Greek, Dutch, and Latin. He studied a variety of topics, including fencing, music, art, history, and math.

During his time overseas, Adams traveled all over Europe. He lived in France, the Netherlands, and Great Britain. He learned to speak French so well that Adams was asked to become the translator for Francis Dana, the U.S. representative to Russia. French was the language used to discuss politics in Russia, and Adams spent nearly two years living there.

John Quincy Adams was elected the sixth president of the United States.

In 1783, Adams returned to France to join his father. In France, he saw the signing of the **Treaty** of Paris. This agreement ended the Revolutionary War. American colonists had won their freedom from British rule.

Once the treaty was signed, Adams returned to the United States to finish his education. He attended Harvard College. After graduating, Adams moved to Massachusetts to study law. In 1790, he opened his own law practice. Adams had few clients and did not enjoy his work. He gave up his practice and decided to serve in politics.

War broke out between Great Britain and France in 1793. President George Washington did not want to take sides in the conflict. He did not want to risk angering either of these powerful nations. Adams wrote several articles supporting Washington's decision. As a reward, Washington asked Adams to be the United States' political minister to the Netherlands. Several years later, his father, President John Adams, would ask Adams to serve as United States' political minister to Prussia.

JOHN ADAMS

John Adams was born in the Massachusetts Bay Colony in 1735. He attended Harvard College, where he earned his law degree. He later became one of the Founding Fathers in America's fight for independence.

During the Revolutionary War, he was a diplomat in France and Holland. In 1783, he helped end the war by negotiating the Treaty of Paris. He then returned to the United States and was elected the country's first vice president under George Washington. He was elected president after Washington left office.

Adams died on July 4, 1826, the 50th anniversary of the signing of the Declaration of Independence. It was the same day that Thomas Jefferson passed away.

The Battle of Bunker Hill was fought near John Quincy Adams' home in Massachusetts.

Adams' Political Career and Legacy

> "America does not go abroad in search of monsters to destroy. She is the well-wisher to freedom and independence of all. She is the champion and vindicator only of her own."
>
> *John Quincy Adams*

In 1814, President James Madison asked John Quincy Adams to help negotiate a treaty with Great Britain. The United States had been at war with Great Britain for two years. Neither side could claim victory, but both countries wanted to end the bloodshed. Adams helped arrange the Treaty of Ghent, which ended the War of 1812.

A few years later, President Monroe asked Adams to be his secretary of state. In his new position, Adams negotiated the Adams-Onís Treaty with Spain in 1819. This agreement gave Spanish-owned land in Florida to the United States for a sum of $5 million. Spain gave up its claim to lands in Oregon Country as well.

In 1824, Adams ran for president, along with three other candidates. They were all from the Democratic-Republican Party. Andrew Jackson, a war hero during the War of 1812, received the most electoral votes. He had 99 of 261 possible votes. Adams was second with 84. William Crawford received 41, and Henry Clay had 37 votes. No one candidate received more than half of the electoral votes, so there was no winner. The 12th **Amendment** stated that the U.S. House of Representatives would

British and U.S. representatives signed the Treaty of Ghent in 1814 to end the War of 1812.

then decide the election, with each state having one vote.

Clay convinced his supporters to vote for Adams. With Clay's help, Adams won the election. Later, Adams named Clay his secretary of state. Jackson and his supporters claimed Adams stole the election through a corrupt bargain. They thought Clay agreed to support Adams because he had offered Clay a governmental post. However, Clay likely supported Adams because they shared similar political views.

During his administration, Adams proposed many improvements to the United States. He supported a national university and a national bank. He wanted to build a system of roads, railroads, and canals. He argued for the development of the arts and sciences. Few people supported Adams' ideas at the time. He had a strong opponent in Jackson, who often disagreed with Adams' policies.

In the 1828 presidential election, Adams faced Jackson again. This time, the results were different. Jackson easily won. Despite his defeat, Adams continued to serve in the government. He spent the next 17 years as a member of the U.S. House of Representatives.

Adams continued to support the arts and sciences. He convinced Congress to accept a $500,000 gift from James Smithson of Great Britain. The money was used to create the Smithsonian Institution, an establishment of learning.

During his time in government, Adams openly opposed slavery. In 1841, he agreed to defend slaves in a **mutiny** case.

A group of Africans were sold illegally to Spanish plantation owners. The slaves rebelled while aboard the slave ship *Amistad*. They killed two crew members and demanded to be returned home. Before reaching Africa, they were captured and sent to prison in Connecticut. The Spanish plantation owners demanded the slaves back. Adams argued to the U.S. Supreme Court that anyone who escaped illegal bondage should be considered free. He won the case, and the Africans were returned home.

Adams may have served only one term as president, but he is remembered for his long years of governmental service. On February 23, 1848, Adams died. He was 80 years old.

Coins are minted to honor former presidents.

The Monroe Doctrine

> **"The American continents …are henceforth not to be considered as subjects for future colonization by any European powers."**
>
> *From the Monroe Doctrine*

The Monroe Doctrine is one of President James Monroe's best-known achievements. Yet, he could not have authored this document without John Quincy Adams, who was secretary of state at the time. Adams helped craft the main ideas behind the Monroe Doctrine.

The Monroe Doctrine was created in reaction to two political problems. Spain was declining in power. Many of its colonies in Latin America had rebelled and become independent. Other European countries, such as Austria, France, and Prussia, were concerned that their own colonies would do the same. The United States feared these nations would send troops to help Spain regain its colonies in Latin America. The United States was concerned that these European powers would create new colonies in North and South America.

In addition, Russia wanted to expand its colonies along the northwest coast of North America. Adams felt that the Americas, both North and South, should not be further colonized by European countries.

Great Britain did not want other European countries colonizing or interfering in the Americas. The British had good trade relations with

James Monroe, author of the Monroe Doctrine, served as the fifth president of the United States.

Latin America. In 1823, the British proposed that the United States and Great Britain form an alliance to end European intervention and colonization in the Western Hemisphere.

Everyone in Monroe's **Cabinet** liked the idea except for Adams. He did not want the United States to keep following Great Britain's lead. He said they should act independently. Adams worried that Great Britain would make the United States agree not to acquire any more territory. Adams wanted this option to remain open to the United States. Monroe agreed with his secretary of state.

In a speech given to Congress on December 2, 1823, Monroe said that Europe would not be allowed to interfere with any of its former colonies in the Americas. The United States would not allow any new colonies to be established. President Monroe promised that the United States would not interfere with the affairs of European countries. In return, he said European countries should not interfere with the

affairs of the United States. To do so would be considered a hostile act.

Even though Adams contributed greatly to what Monroe said, the ideas in this speech became known as the Monroe Doctrine. It helped prove to the world that the United States was a strong, independent nation.

President James Monroe wrote a letter to former President Thomas Jefferson. Monroe was seeking advice on a proposed alliance with Great Britain that would put an end to European colonization in the Americas.

Andrew Jackson's Early Years

Andrew Jackson was born on March 15, 1767, in Waxhaw, South Carolina. Andrew had a difficult childhood. His father died shortly before he was born. His oldest brother, Hugh, died while fighting in the Revolutionary War. In 1781, his other brother, Robert, died of smallpox. When Andrew was 14 years old, his mother died of **cholera**. Andrew, now an orphan, was raised by relatives.

Growing up, Andrew went to frontier schools. These small, one-room schools often lacked basic supplies. One great advantage Andrew gained from going to school was learning how to read. Many adults where he lived did not have this skill.

At age 13, Jackson joined the Continental Army to fight the British in the Revolutionary War. During the war, he was captured. When a

British officer ordered Jackson to clean his boots, Jackson refused. The officer hit him with the dull side of his sword, leaving a permanent scar on Jackson's forehead. Jackson is the only president to have been a prisoner of war.

After the war, Jackson studied law in North Carolina, then moved to Tennessee. From 1798–1804, he served as a judge on the Tennessee Supreme Court.

Jackson was the only president who fought in both the Revolutionary War and the War of 1812. During the War of 1812, he was appointed major general of the volunteer corps, a group of Tennessee soldiers. Jackson led them against the Creek Indians. The British were helping American Indians rebel against the United States. The American Indians did not want American settlers

Andrew Jackson served as a major general during the War of 1812.

to take their lands. In October 1813, some Creeks attacked Fort Mims in what is now Alabama. A few weeks later, Jackson defeated the Creeks.

Jackson was eventually promoted to major general. Then, in 1815, he and his troops successfully defended the city of New Orleans against attacking British forces. More than 2,000 British soldiers were killed, wounded, or captured. Jackson lost only eight men, and 13 were wounded. The lopsided victory made him a national hero.

Jackson and his troops did not know the war had ended before the Battle of New Orleans. The United States and Great Britain signed the Treaty of Ghent.

Jackson retired from the military in 1821 and moved to Tennessee. Two years later, he was elected to the U.S. Senate.

"It was settled by the Constitution, the laws, and the whole practice of the government that the entire executive power is vested in the President of the United States."
Andrew Jackson

Andrew Jackson led U.S. forces to victory during the Battle of New Orleans.

Jackson's Presidency

In 1824, Jackson ran for the presidency. As a war hero, he was a very popular candidate. Even though Jackson received the most electoral votes, he did not receive enough votes to win. The election had to be decided by the U.S. House of Representatives, which elected John Quincy Adams. Jackson's ambition to be president, however, did not end there. Four years later, Jackson easily defeated Adams to become the seventh president of the United States. He was re-elected in 1832.

During his eight-year presidency, Jackson dealt with two major issues. First, was the Nullification Crisis. It began when Jackson's vice president, John Calhoun, said that any state could refuse to obey a federal law if it did not agree with the law.

Calhoun supported states' rights. Like many Southerners, he believed that states should have the power to govern themselves. On the other side of the issue were people who believed in a strong central government.

Andrew Jackson followed John Quincy Adams into office and served as the seventh president of the United States.

They felt the federal government should have power over the states. This disagreement would divide the country for many years.

At the time, many southern states were upset with the high **tariffs**, or taxes on imported goods. They had to pay these tariffs to the federal government. In 1832, South Carolina passed an Ordinance of Nullification, which stated that the federal government could not collect tariffs in South Carolina. Jackson supported states' rights, but he feared that South Carolina would secede, or leave, the Union. Jackson posted troops along South Carolina's borders and threatened to collect the taxes using force. Eventually, a compromise was reached. The Tariff Act of 1833 lowered the tariffs states had to pay.

The other major issue that Jackson dealt with was a personal battle with the Second Bank of the United States. Congress had created the First Bank of the United States in 1791. It served as the federal government's main bank and was the only bank used for federal funds. The bank's **charter** ended in 1811. Five years later, Congress created the Second Bank of the United States. Its charter ended in 1836.

Jackson believed that the bank had too much power. He thought it kept money in the hands of the rich and did not benefit working-class people. When Congress voted to extend the bank's charter, Jackson **vetoed** the bill. He took money out of the federal bank and deposited it in state banks. Jackson

> "As long as our government is administered for the good of the people, and is regulated by their will; as long as it secures to us the rights of persons and of property, liberty of conscience and of the press, it will be worth defending."
> *Andrew Jackson*

let the Second Bank of the United States's charter expire in 1836. Many people believe Jackson's actions led to the Panic of 1837, a time of economic decline.

DEMOCRATIC PARTY

Andrew Jackson is considered one of the founding fathers of the Democratic Party. By the time of the presidential election in 1824, there was one national party, the Democratic-Republican Party.

The controversy surrounding the 1824 presidential election caused Jackson and his supporters to split from the Democratic-Republicans. Jackson emerged as leader of the Jacksonians. This party was a strong supporter of states' rights.

Jackson created the national convention process, which nominates presidential candidates for political parties. The Jacksonians held their first national convention in 1832 and nominated Jackson. In 1844, the party changed its name to the Democratic Party.

Jackson's Achievements and Legacy

> "Each public officer who takes an oath to support the Constitution swears that he will support it as he understands it, and not as it is understood by others."
>
> *Andrew Jackson*

As president, Andrew Jackson achieved many successes. He expanded the power of the presidential office because he believed that the president was the only representative to all citizens of the United States. During his time in office, Jackson vetoed more than a dozen pieces of legislation. This was more than the first six presidents combined. Before Jackson, presidents only vetoed bills that they thought were unconstitutional. Jackson vetoed bills that he did not agree with.

A statue near the U.S. Capitol honors Andrew Jackson for his years of service, both as a military and a political leader.

Jackson forced out members of his Cabinet who refused to carry out his orders. He wanted to make sure that the Cabinet was united in pursuing his goals.

One of Jackson's greatest achievements was elimination of the national debt. The United States had borrowed money from foreign governments to support itself during the Revolutionary War and the War of 1812. On January 8, 1835, the federal government paid off its debt completely for the first time in its history.

Toward the end of his presidency, Jackson recognized the Republic of Texas' independence. This country, which is now the state of Texas, won its independence from Mexico in 1836. Many Americans lived in Texas. Sam Houston, a friend of Jackson's and the former governor of Tennessee, was the president of the republic. Jackson hoped that Texas would eventually become a state in the Union.

Jackson did not run for a third term as president. Instead, he supported Martin Van Buren, who won the presidency in 1836. However, Jackson continued to offer his advice to members of the Democratic Party.

Jackson had a great influence on modern politics. Not only did he help create the Democratic Party, he worked to convince Americans that their votes were important. The number of American voters increased from 1.5 million in 1836 to 2.4 million in 1840. This is the largest increase between elections in U.S. history. Eighty percent of eligible voters voted in 1840, compared to 60 percent in the three previous elections.

Jackson encouraged more citizens to get involved in politics. He believed that public offices should be rotated among party supporters, also known as the spoils system. This meant that the winning party in a presidential election would remove current members of the opposing party from the Cabinet. Jackson believed that any party supporter could work in public office because it did not require special training.

On June 8, 1845, Jackson passed away at his home in Tennessee. He was 78 years old.

Samuel Houston served as the first president of the Republic of Texas.

Martin Van Buren's Early Years

> "The framers of our excellent Constitution… wisely judged that the less Government interferes with private pursuits the better for general prosperity."
>
> *Martin Van Buren*

Martin Van Buren was born on December 5, 1782, in Kinderhook, New York. He would be the first president who was born an American citizen. All previous presidents were born in places that were not yet part of the United States.

Van Buren's family owned a tavern that was a popular place for politicians to gather and talk. Growing up in this environment led to Van Buren's interest in politics.

Van Buren attended the village school and an academy until he was 14. Then, he took a job as a law clerk. He could not afford to go to college, so he studied law on his own. He began practicing law in 1803, but soon became very active in state politics as a New York state senator and attorney general.

Van Buren had an active career in politics. In 1820, he was elected to the U.S. Senate. He later served as governor of New York. In 1829, he resigned as governor to become President Andrew Jackson's secretary of state.

Jackson and Van Buren quickly became good friends. In 1833, Van Buren became Jackson's vice president, and in 1836, Jackson supported Van Buren's run for the presidency. He defeated the leading **Whig candidate**, William Henry Harrison.

Many saw Van Buren as Jackson's successor. In his inaugural address, he even promised to follow in Jackson's

Martin Van Buren served as a U.S senator and governor of New York before being elected to the presidency.

footsteps. Van Buren kept all but one member of Jackson's Cabinet. He replaced Secretary of War Lewis Cass.

Van Buren took office during the Panic of 1837. A year earlier, Jackson had shut down the Second Bank of the United States. He had moved funds from the federal bank to small state banks. The state banks used these funds to print and loan money to businesses and citizens. They gave out too much money. **Inflation** rose, which caused U.S. money to lose its value. As a result, many foreign investors did not want to accept American currency anymore. They were also asking to be repaid for the money they had loaned to American businesses.

During this time, more than 800 banks shut down, and many businesses closed. People lost their life savings. Ten percent of American workers were unemployed. Businesses had to lower their wages, and the crisis did not end for nearly six years.

Whig Party leaders complained that Van Buren did not do enough to help the country during the Panic of 1837. Van Buren did pass the Independent Treasury Act in 1840. It set up a federal banking system operated by the government. Van Buren hoped this banking system would prevent any similar economic problems, but the Panic of 1837 would continue to cause him problems.

The Second Bank of the United States is located in Philadelphia, Pennsylvania.

Martin Van Buren's Presidency

> "Is it possible to be anything in this country without being a politician?"
>
> *Martin Van Buren*

During Martin Van Buren's presidency, the United States forced the Cherokee Indians to move from their lands in the southeast to the territory that is now the state of Oklahoma. Southern states wanted Cherokee land to grow cotton. To convince the Cherokee to move, the United States offered to buy their land in Tennessee, Alabama, North Carolina, and Georgia for $5 million. The United States agreed to pay for the cost of their relocation to a new territory, which would be called Indian Territory. The United States would give the Cherokee Indians two years to make this move.

Before Van Buren's presidency, U.S. government officials and several members of the Cherokee Nation met in New Echota, Georgia. They signed the Treaty of New Echota, which finalized the agreement with the Cherokee. The Cherokee, however, argued that official representatives of their nation never signed the treaty. As a result, they refused to obey the agreement.

In May of 1838, Van Buren ordered the U.S. Army to force more than 16,000 Cherokee to leave their land. The Cherokee were forced to march to their new home, which was 1,000 miles away. They had little food, but they continued to march through a brutally cold winter. During the long march, nearly 4,000 Cherokee died. By March of 1839, all of those who survived the long winter arrived in Indian Territory. The path from their homeland to the new land became known as the Trail of Tears because of the struggles the Cherokee had endured.

Another issue that marred Van Buren's presidency was the **annexation** of Texas. The year Van Buren took office, the Republic of Texas won its independence from Mexico.

Martin Van Buren served as the eighth president of the United States.

Texans and many Southerners wanted Texas to become part of the United States. Texas allowed slavery, and Southerners wanted another slave state to join the Union. That would strengthen their support for slavery.

Van Buren supported Southern views, but he feared Texas' statehood would make the conflict worse. Van Buren worried that, with another slave state in the Union, the issue of slavery would further divide the country. He joined Northerners in opposing Texas' statehood. His opposition angered his biggest supporter, Andrew Jackson.

Without Jackson's support and because of the Panic of 1837, Van Buren was not re-elected in 1840. He lost the election to William Henry Harrison.

Van Buren ran again for office in 1844, but he lost to James Polk. He then helped form the Free-Soil Party. This party was made up of Democrats and Whigs who opposed slavery. He was the party's candidate for president in the 1948 election but lost to Zachary Taylor.

Eventually, Van Buren rejoined the Democratic Party, but he continued to oppose slavery. Van Buren died in Kinderhook on July 24, 1862. He was 79 years old.

THE WHIG PARTY

The Whig Party was formed in 1834 to oppose Andrew Jackson and his Democratic Party. It contained the remaining members of the Democratic-Republican Party as well as members from other small political parties. This party was led by Henry Clay of Kentucky and Daniel Webster of Massachusetts.

Clay lost the 1832 and 1844 presidential elections. Whig Party member William Henry Harrison became president in 1841, and Zachary Taylor won the 1848 election.

The party disintegrated after the presidential election of 1856, however. The main cause was the slavery issue. Northern Whigs were in favor of ending slavery and preventing it from spreading to new territories. Southern Whigs wanted states to be able to decide whether to allow slavery or not. Most of the Southern Whigs eventually joined the Democratic Party, while Northerners joined the new Republican Party.

American Indians have re-enacted the 1,000-mile journey of the Cherokee Indians to honor their suffering.

William Henry Harrison

William Henry Harrison was born on February 9, 1773, in Charles City County, Virginia. He was the youngest of seven children born to Benjamin Harrison, one of the signers of the Declaration of Independence. Harrison's father served as governor of Virginia from 1781 to 1784.

> **"I contend that the strongest of all governments is that which is most free."**
> *William Henry Harrison*

At first, Harrison wanted to be a doctor. He studied medicine for several years. After his father died in 1791, he soon ran out of money. He then gave up the idea of becoming a doctor and joined the military.

Harrison was assigned to protect settlers in the Northwest Territory. This area is now the states of Ohio, Illinois, Michigan, Indiana, and Wisconsin. Later, Harrison served as governor of Indiana Territory. During this time, Harrison arranged several treaties with American Indians that opened up land to white settlers. However, not all American Indians agreed with these treaties.

Two Shawnee brothers, Tecumseh and the Prophet, formed a confederacy of Indian Nations. This group fought against settlers on their land. In 1811, while Tecumseh was away, Harrison and his troops attacked the Indian Confederacy at Prophetstown. This village was near the mouth of the Tippecanoe River in the state of Indiana. Harrison defeated the American Indians, who had been armed with British weapons.

The next year, the War of 1812 began. Harrison served as an army general. He led his troops against British and American Indian forces in a battle at the Thames River. Tecumseh was killed during this battle.

William Henry Harrison was elected the ninth president of the United States but served only one month in office.

After the War of 1812, Harrison entered politics. He served in the U.S. House of Representatives from 1816 to 1819. He was elected to the U.S. Senate in 1825. In 1828, President John Quincy Adams asked him to be the United States' political minister to Colombia.

Harrison joined the Whig Party and ran for president in the 1836 election. He lost to Martin Van Buren. Harrison had better luck during the next election. In 1840, he denied Van Buren his re-election bid. Harrison was the first Whig elected to be president.

Harrison had been in office for one month, when he caught a cold. His cold developed into pneumonia. On April 4, 1841, he died, becoming the first president to die in office. He served the shortest time of any president. Vice President John Tyler became president after Harrison's death.

TECUMSEH'S CURSE

Legend has it that either Tecumseh or his brother spoke a curse that would kill every president elected in a year ending in zero. The first victim was William Henry Harrison, whose troops killed Tecumseh in 1813. Harrison died of pneumonia after serving only 31 days in office.

Victims of Tecumseh's Curse

- William Henry Harrison (1840)–died of pneumonia
- Abraham Lincoln (1860)–assassinated
- James Garfield (1880)–assassinated
- William McKinley (1900)–assassinated
- Warren Harding (1920)–died of a stroke
- Franklin Roosevelt (1940)–died of a cerebral hemorrhage
- John Kennedy (1960)–assassinated

Ronald Reagan (1980) ended the curse when he survived an attempted assassination.

Shawnee leader Tecumseh organized an Indian Confederacy to oppose the settlement of American Indian lands. He was killed at the Battle of the Thames River during the War of 1812.

John Tyler

"Wealth can only be accumulated by the earnings of industry and the savings of frugality." *John Tyler*

John Tyler was born in Charles City County, Virginia, on March 29, 1790. Tyler's father was governor of Virginia. Tyler was destined to be involved in politics. At the young age of 21, he was elected to the Virginia state legislature.

In 1816, Tyler was elected to the U.S. House of Representatives. After two terms, he returned to serve on the Virginia state legislature. He then followed his father's footsteps and became governor of Virginia.

Tyler was originally a supporter of President Andrew Jackson. He believed in states' rights and opposed the Second Bank of the United States. He later became a Jackson opponent. Tyler did not agree with how Jackson handled of the Nullification Crisis and threats of secession.

Tyler joined the Whig party, which was created to oppose Jackson. During the 1840 presidential election, Tyler was selected as the Whig's vice presidential candidate to run alongside William Henry Harrison.

After Harrison's death, people did not know if Tyler should become president or if he should hold the office until a new election could take place.

John Tyler became the 10th president of the United States after William Henry Harrison's death. He was the first vice president to assume office through the death of a president.

However, Tyler assumed the presidency and became the first vice president to take office because of the death of a president.

As president, one of the largest issues Tyler faced was the creation of the Third National Bank. He believed its creation was unconstitutional. Tyler felt the bank would infringe on the rights of state banks. U.S. Senator Henry Clay and the rest of the Whigs wanted a new national bank, but Tyler vetoed their attempts. As a result, everyone in the Cabinet resigned except for Daniel Webster. The Whig Party expelled Tyler from the party.

Despite these difficulties, Tyler had great success in dealing with foreign affairs. In 1842, he agreed to the Webster-Ashburton Treaty with Great Britain. This agreement established the border between Maine and Canada. He signed a treaty with China, which allowed the two countries to begin trading with each other. However, his attempts to annex the Republic of Texas failed because of the Whigs' opposition.

Tyler did not have the support of a major political party, so he knew he could not win re-election. He gave his support to James Polk in the 1844 election. Polk wanted to make Texas part of the Union. Once Polk was elected, Congress voted to approve the annexation of Texas. Tyler signed the resolution three days before his term ended. Texas became the 28th state. On his final day in office, Tyler signed legislation that made Florida the 27th state.

After his time in office, Tyler and his family moved back to Virginia. He died on January 18, 1862, at the age of 71.

Senator Henry Clay (pictured) and the Whigs expelled John Tyler from the Whig Party after he vetoed a bill to create the Third National Bank of the United States.

James Polk

> **"Foreign powers do not seem to appreciate the true character of our government."**
> *James Polk*

James K. Polk was born November 2, 1795, in Mecklenburg County, North Carolina. As a child, he moved with his family to the frontier state of Tennessee. Polk received formal instruction at a Presbyterian school outside Columbia, Tennessee, before enrolling at the University of North Carolina in 1816. After graduating, he studied law in hopes of entering politics.

Polk became a member of the U.S. House of Representatives in 1825, and he served as Speaker of the House from 1835 to 1839. He left the House of Representatives to become governor of Tennessee.

Polk was a leading contender for the Democratic nomination for vice president in the 1844 election. Former president Martin Van Buren was expected to win the nomination for president. During his time in Congress, Polk had become friends with Andrew Jackson. Jackson no longer supported Van Buren, and he helped Polk win the presidential nomination instead. George Dallas from Pennsylvania won the vice presidential nomination.

One of the biggest issues surrounding the election was expanding the United States farther west. Southern states were in favor of adding Texas because they wanted another slave state in the Union. Northern states were in favor of having Oregon join the Union because it would be a free state.

Polk believed strongly that the Republic of Texas and the Oregon Territory should both become part of the United States. He even wanted to acquire California from Mexico. His Whig opponent in the 1844 election, Henry Clay, did not support making Texas a state. This led Southerners to believe that Clay would try to stop the spread of slavery, so they supported Polk.

James Polk was elected the 11th president of the United States.

Polk won the election. As president, he had four goals, all of which he achieved. He wanted to reduce tariffs and establish an independent treasury for federal funds. He wanted to settle the Oregon border dispute with Great Britain and to acquire California.

To acquire California, Polk went to war with Mexico. He threatened to do the same with Great Britain for control of Oregon. In 1846, the Oregon Treaty established the western border between Canada and the United States. Oregon Territory became the states of Washington and Oregon.

Polk did not run for office in 1848. Instead, he returned to Tennessee to retire. He died June 15, 1849, at the age of 53.

MANIFEST DESTINY

The term *Manifest Destiny* was first used in 1845. It was coined by magazine editor John L. O'Sullivan, who wrote that it was the United States' destiny to expand. Manifest Destiny is the belief that the United States was destined to expand from the Atlantic to the Pacific coasts. Those who favored Manifest Destiny believed that expansion was good for the United States, even if it meant using force to acquire new lands. The Democrats favored this concept, while the Whigs rejected the idea. Polk used Manifest Destiny to justify the United States' acquisitions of Oregon, Texas, New Mexico, and California.

United States Territorial Acquisitions

The Acquisitions of Oregon, Texas, California, and New Mexico

The United States continued to expand throughout the 1800s. It began with the Louisiana Purchase and the purchase of Spanish-owned land in Florida. The expansion would continue until all of the land in the continental 48 states was acquired.

In 1846, the United States signed a treaty with Great Britain. This agreement divided Oregon Territory at the 49th parallel, which is an imaginary line to show the distance from the equator. Land north of this line became the Canadian province of British Columbia. Land south of the line became the states of Oregon and Washington.

Texas, California, and New Mexico were originally part of the Mexican Republic. Americans began to settle in Texas in the 1820s. Many of these settlers did not want to be ruled by the Mexican government. They rebelled in 1836. Several small battles followed. Mexican forces arrived in San Antonio in early 1836 to try to put an end to the rebellion. Texan troops, numbering 189 men, took cover at the Alamo, a former religious mission. About 4,000 Mexican soldiers attacked the Alamo. It took them 13 days to defeat the Texans.

Davy Crockett was one of the legendary defenders of the Alamo.

Victory in the Mexican War led to the United States adding several territories.

Using the rallying cry, "Remember the Alamo," General Sam Houston led his troops against Mexican forces in the Battle of San Jacinto. The battle lasted only minutes, and hundreds of Mexican soldiers were either killed or captured. The Texans captured Mexican General Antonio Lopez de Santa Anna and made him sign a treaty that gave Texas its independence. Despite this agreement, Mexico did not recognize Texas' independence.

The newly formed Texan government applied to become part of the United States. President Martin Van Buren and his Cabinet declined its entry since it would mean going to war with Mexico. The northern states opposed Texas joining the United States. They feared Texas would become a slave state.

Texas remained an independent republic for the next nine years. Then, James Polk was elected to the presidency. He wanted to annex Texas. In December 1845, Congress voted to admit Texas into the Union. This action led to the Mexican War.

Even though the American troops were outnumbered, they defeated the more powerful Mexican army in nearly every battle. The war ended in 1848, with the Treaty of Guadalupe Hidalgo. In addition to Texas, this agreement gave the New Mexico and California Territories to the United States. In return, the United States paid Mexico $15 million.

"The Oregon [matter] and the annexation of Texas are now all-important to the security and future peace and prosperity of our union, and I hope there are a sufficient number of pure American democrats to carry into effect the annexation of Texas and [extension of] our laws over Oregon. No temporizing policy or all is lost." *Andrew Jackson, in a letter to Francis P. Blair*

Zachary Taylor

> "I have always done my duty. I am ready to die. My only regret is for the friends I leave behind me."
>
> *Zachary Taylor*

Zachary Taylor was born in Orange County, Virginia, on November 24, 1784. His family moved to a plantation in the frontier state of Kentucky. Taylor did not have a formal education because there were no schools nearby.

Taylor joined the U.S. Army when he was 23 years old and spent 40 years in the service. He was promoted to major because of his successful defense of Fort Harrison, Indiana, in the War of 1812. He fought in several American Indian Wars. He helped defeat the Sac and Fox Indians in the Black Hawk War of 1832. During the second Seminole War that took place between 1837 and 1840, Seminole Indians wanted to remove European settlers from their land in Florida. Taylor helped to end the American Indian resistance to the settlers.

As a general in the Mexican War, Taylor had several major victories. At the Battle of Buena Vista, his troops were outnumbered by a stronger and more experienced Mexican army led by General Antonio Lopez de Santa Anna. Despite the odds, Taylor led his troops to victory and became a national hero. Due to his popularity, the Whigs nominated him to run against Democrat Lewis Cass in the 1848 election.

States' rights was the most dominant issue in those days. Cass was in favor of letting the citizens of each new state have the right to decide whether they wanted to allow slavery. Many assumed that Taylor, who was a slaveholder himself, would support the same pro-slavery position. Northern states disliked

Zachary Taylor was elected the 12th president of the United States.

both candidates and formed the Free-Soil Party. They nominated Martin Van Buren as their presidential candidate.

Taylor won in a close election. He received only 47 percent of the popular vote, but he won a majority of the electoral votes. He became the first president to be elected with no prior political experience.

New Mexico and California wanted to be admitted into the Union. These territories were settled by Northerners who took an abolitionist stance and opposed slavery. Southern states thought Taylor would refuse their entry into the United States. However, Taylor suggested that New Mexico and California develop their own constitutions before applying to become states.

Taylor's approach angered southern states. During a conference with Taylor in 1850, their leaders threatened secession. Taylor said that he would do everything in his power to preserve the United States. He warned Southerners that if they seceded, he would hang them, like he had done with deserters and spies during the Mexican War.

Later that year, at the 4th of July ceremonies at the Washington Monument, Taylor became sick. He died five days later at the age of 65. His vice president, Millard Fillmore, took office.

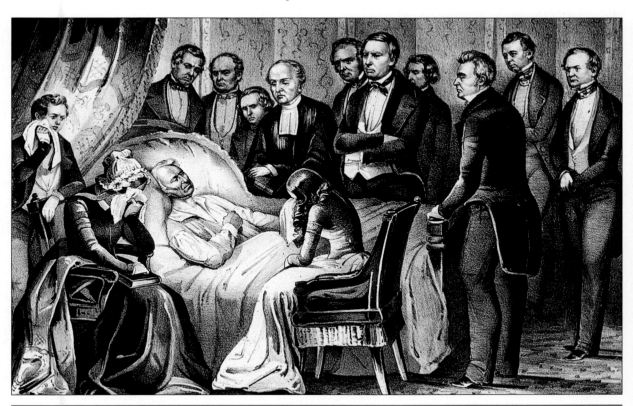

After less than two years in office, Zachary Taylor fell ill and died.

Millard Fillmore

> "Let us remember that revolutions do not always establish freedom. Our own free institutions were not the offspring of our revolution. They existed before."
>
> *Millard Fillmore*

Millard Fillmore was born in Cayuga County, New York, on January 7, 1800. As a young boy, Fillmore worked on his father's farm. His family was poor, so he became a cloth maker's apprentice as a teenager to help support his family.

Fillmore attended one-room schools during his childhood, but mainly educated himself. He read as many books as possible. Fillmore studied law during his youth. He opened his own practice in New York in 1823.

Years later, Fillmore joined the Whig Party. He was elected to the U.S. House of Representatives in 1833 and served for eight years. He became chairman of the powerful Ways and Means Committee. This committee helps decide how the government gets money through taxes and tariffs.

At the Whig National Convention in 1848, Fillmore was nominated to be Zachary Taylor's running mate. Taylor won but died two years later. Fillmore became president after Taylor's death.

The issue of slavery continued to divide the United States. When California wanted to become a state, Henry Clay created the Compromise of 1850. He hoped this agreement would resolve the slavery issue and keep southern states from seceding. In this agreement, California would become a free state. In return, the South got a law called the Fugitive Slave Law. This law stated that slaves escaping to the North would be returned to their owners.

Taylor was against the Compromise of 1850, but Fillmore supported it. After Taylor's death, Fillmore signed it into law.

After Taylor's death, Vice President Millard Fillmore became the 13th president of the United States.

He believed that the agreement was necessary to ease the tensions between the North and the South.

The Compromise of 1850 included other laws. Buying and selling slaves in Washington, D.C., became illegal. Those who currently owned slaves could keep them, but no one could buy or sell new slaves. The land acquired from Mexico as a result of the Mexican War was divided into two states, New Mexico and Utah.

The Compromise of 1850 stated that these states could decide for themselves whether they wanted to allow slavery.

Fillmore's support of the Compromise of 1850 angered many Whigs. As a result, he did not win their nomination at the Whig National Convention in 1852. Fillmore tried running for president again in 1856 but lost the election. He retired to New York and died March 8, 1874. He was 74 years old.

The Compromise of 1850 made slave auctions illegal in Washington, D.C.

Franklin Pierce

Franklin Pierce was born on November 23, 1804, in Hillsborough, New Hampshire. His parents were wealthy, and he attended private schools until he was 12 years old. At age 15, he entered Bowdoin College in Maine.

After graduation, Pierce studied law and soon opened a law office in Hillsborough. He entered politics in 1829, the same year his father was re-elected governor of New Hampshire. Pierce won a seat on the state legislature and remained there until 1833.

Pierce entered into national politics. He was a strong supporter of President Andrew Jackson and became a Democrat. Pierce was elected to the U.S. House of Representatives in 1833. Three years later, he became a member of the U.S. Senate. At the time, he was the youngest senator in office. He served in the Senate until 1842, when he resigned at the request of his wife, Jane, and moved back home to New Hampshire.

Pierce remained active in politics and soon became the New Hampshire state chair of the Democratic Party. He helped manage James Polk's successful campaign in the 1844 election. That same year, Pierce became a U.S. district attorney for New Hampshire. The following year, he turned down an offer by Polk to join his Cabinet as U.S. Attorney General.

Franklin Pierce was elected the 14th president of the United States.

Pierce briefly left politics to fight in the Mexican War. Even though he had no prior military experience, Pierce quickly rose through the ranks. President Polk made Pierce a colonel, and by the war's end, he was a brigadier general.

When he returned from the war, Pierce resumed his position as head of his state's Democratic Party. At the 1852 Democratic Convention, the four leading presidential candidates were unable to win the two-thirds majority of **delegates** required for the nomination. After 34 tries, they were still deadlocked.

It became clear to Democratic leaders that they needed a new candidate who could appeal to a majority of their voters. Pierce's friends placed his name on the 35th ballot, and he won the nomination on the 49th ballot. He went on to defeat Whig candidate General Winfield Scott, who was Pierce's commander in the Mexican War.

> "A Republic without parties is a complete anomaly. The histories of all popular governments show absurd is the idea of their attempting to exist without parties."
>
> *Franklin Pierce*

General Winfield Scott commanded troops that marched into Mexico during the Mexican War.

Kansas-Nebraska Act

Slavery was a hotly debated issue in the United States. As the country continued to expand westward, Congress debated whether each new territory should allow slavery. The South wanted an equal number of slave and free states so the region would have equal representation in Congress.

In the mid-1850s, the territories of Kansas and Nebraska wanted to be admitted into the Union. Senator Stephen Douglas of Illinois introduced the Kansas-Nebraska bill. It stated that the residents of each territory would decide whether to allow slavery. This law was meant to replace the Missouri Compromise of 1820, which prevented slavery in states north of the longitude line that formed the northern border of Missouri.

Many politicians worried that Douglas' proposal would further divide North and South. A new political party emerged from these worries. Members of the Whig, Northern Democratic, and Free-Soil Parties, who opposed slavery, joined forces to create the Republican Party. They hoped to stop the spread of slavery.

At the time, a majority of Nebraska was occupied by abolitionists. Kansas had a mix of both abolitionists and pro-slavery settlers. The abolitionist movement brought people from as far as Maine to settle in Kansas. Most pro-slavery settlers simply crossed the border from neighboring Missouri. Despite the Republicans' efforts, the Kansas-Nebraska Act of 1854 passed. Violence soon erupted in Kansas between pro-slavery settlers and abolitionists. A series of battles ensued. "Bloody Kansas," as it was called, became a small-scale civil war.

Stephen Douglas introduced the Kansas-Nebraska bill.

Meanwhile, people in Kansas voted to make it a slave state. However, when Kansas applied for entry into the Union, Congress refused. They stated that since Kansas was north of Missouri, it could not be a slave state. Congress still followed the Missouri Compromise of 1820.

The battles within the state continued until 1859, when a state constitution was finally approved. It recognized abolitionist views. Kansas joined the Union in January 1861, just three months before the opening shots of the Civil War.

After his presidency, Pierce retired to Concord, New Hampshire, where he died on October 8, 1869. He was 64 years old.

Pierce was seen as a moderate leader, trying to compromise with both sides on the states' rights issue. Although he was seen as the president who put the United States on track to the Civil War, many argue that the country was already well on its way. No president before him was fully able to resolve the disagreements over slavery.

> **"If a man who has attained this high office cannot free himself from cliques and act independently, our constitution is valueless."** *Franklin Pierce*

After his term in office, Franklin Pierce retired to his home in New Hampshire.

James Buchanan

> ## "What is right and what is practicable are two different things."
>
> *James Buchanan*

James Buchanan was born in Cove Gap, Pennsylvania, on April 23, 1791. He was the second of 11 children. Buchanan's father was an Irish immigrant who became a successful merchant. His mother was a self-educated woman who shared her passion for reading with her children.

In 1796, the family moved to nearby Mercersburg, where they lived above the family general store. Buchanan worked in the store with his father, which helped him learn math and bookkeeping.

Buchanan went to school at the Old Stone Academy in Mercersburg. At the age of 16, he was admitted to Dickinson College, about 70 miles away from his home. He was a mischievous student, and he was nearly expelled from school. However, a family friend helped him get readmitted, and he graduated with honors two years later.

After graduation, Buchanan began studying law, but politics was his true calling. In 1815, he was elected to the Pennsylvania state legislature. A few years later, he was elected to the U.S House of Representatives as a member of the Democratic Party.

James Buchanan was elected the 15th president of the United States.

Buchanan spent 10 years in the House of Representatives. In 1831, President Andrew Jackson appointed him to serve as the U.S. Minister to Russia. After returning to the United States in 1833, he was elected to the U.S. Senate.

During the election in 1844, Buchanan tried to gain the Democratic nomination for president, but he lost to James Polk. After winning the presidential election, Polk appointed Buchanan to be secretary of state. Buchanan helped arrange the annexation of Texas and the Oregon Treaty, among other accomplishments.

In 1852, Buchanan again tried again to win the presidential nomination for the Democratic Party. There was a deadlock between Buchanan and three other candidates. Franklin Pierce was nominated. In 1853, Pierce appointed Buchanan to be the United States' political minister to Great Britain.

Finally, in 1856, Buchanan won the Democratic nomination. He ran against former President Millard Fillmore and John C. Frémont, the first presidential candidate of the newly organized Republican Party. Although the combined popular vote of his two opponents was greater than his, Buchanan won the election. He received 174 of the 296 electoral votes.

President James Buchanan chose his Cabinet members after winning the presidency in 1856.

On the Brink of War

The slavery debate continued to dominate the political scene in the mid-1800s. Like Franklin Pierce before him, Buchanan did not take a firm stance on either side of the issue. However, he believed that it was best if the people in each state and territory decided whether they wanted to allow slavery.

Two days after his inauguration, the U.S. Supreme Court handed down the Dred Scott decision. Scott was a Missouri slave whose owner moved to the free state of Illinois and then to the free state of Wisconsin. Since he was living in a free state, Scott said he should be a free man. The Supreme Court disagreed. It stated that the Constitution did not recognize slaves as U.S. citizens, so they did not have the same rights. Scott did not have the right to sue for his freedom. A slave was considered property, and property was protected and guaranteed by the Constitution.

In this same ruling, the Supreme Court stated that the Missouri Compromise was unconstitutional. It said that slavery could not be banned in new territories or states. This decision further divided the North and the South. Abolitionists were upset, while Southerners applauded the ruling.

In 1860, near the end of Buchanan's presidency, South Carolina voted to secede from the United States.

Dred Scott tried to fight for his freedom in the U.S. Supreme Court.

> **"Let us look the danger fairly in the face. Secession is neither more nor less than revolution."**
>
> *James Buchanan*

Although Buchanan said that secession was wrong, he stated that he could not stop any state from doing so.

South Carolina issued a document on why it voted to secede. At the top of the list was the claim that northern states were not following the Fugitive Slave Law.

Buchanan tried to find some middle ground between free states and the slave states, but he had little success. Before leaving office, six more southern states seceded. All of the Southerners in Buchanan's Cabinet resigned.

Buchanan angered the South when he refused to order U.S. troops out of Fort Sumter in Charleston, South Carolina. On January 5, 1861, Buchanan sent a ship to carry military supplies to Fort Sumter. Four days later, South Carolina troops opened fire on the ship, forcing it to turn around. Buchanan did nothing in reaction to this.

Many historians considered Buchanan a talented and skillful politician. He was honest and had excellent legal abilities. However, many people blamed him for leading the country to the Civil War. He did nothing as southern states began to secede. Buchanan died in his home June 1, 1868. He was 77 years old.

The first shot of the Civil War would be fired at Fort Sumter, one month after James Buchanan left office.

Timeline

The Expansion and Reform Era was a time of change and growth in the United States. New political parties were formed, many new laws were passed, and wars were fought. With the War of 1812 and the Monroe Doctrine, the United States proved that it was a

1800s	1810s	1820s
PRESIDENTS		
In 1800, Thomas Jefferson is elected to be the third president of the United States. James Madison is elected to the presidency in 1808.	 James Monroe is elected to the presidency in 1816.	In 1823, John Quincy Adams is elected to be the sixth president of the United states. Andrew Jackson wins the presidency in 1828.
UNITED STATES		
In 1803, President Jefferson arranges the Louisiana Purchase. 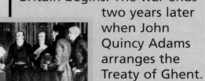	The War of 1812 with Great Britain begins. The war ends two years later when John Quincy Adams arranges the Treaty of Ghent.	In 1823, President James Monroe gives a speech, which becomes known as the Monroe Doctrine.
WORLD		
Spain joins French leader Napoleon Bonaparte in his war against Great Britain.	Napoleon surrenders at Waterloo on June 18, 1815. 	Mexico wins its independence from Spain.

world power to be reckoned with. It kept European countries from further colonizing the Americas. The United States nearly tripled in size, beginning with the Louisiana Purchase. Presidents during this time were very successful in negotiating for land from other countries. When talk failed, U.S. leaders were not afraid to go to war to obtain land. The southwestern United States was won from Mexico during the Mexican War.

1830s	1840s	1850s
PRESIDENTS		
Jackson wins re-election in 1832 but does not run in 1936. Martin Van Buren is elected the eighth president of the United States.	In 1840, William Henry Harrison is elected the ninth president of the United States. He is the first Whig candidate to win the presidency. He also is the first president to die in office. John Tyler then becomes the United States 10th president.	In 1850, Millard Fillmore takes office after President Zachary Taylor dies. 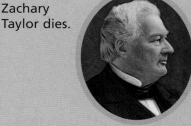
UNITED STATES		
In 1838, Cherokee Indians begin their long march to Indian Territory. The path they took would later be called the Trail of Tears because of the hardships the Cherokee American Indians endured.	In 1846, the United States annexes Texas. 	The Compromise of 1850 is signed into law. It allows California to enter the Union and contains the Fugitive Slave Law.
WORLD		
British Parliament passes the Slavery Abolition Act in 1833. All British-owned slaves are given their freedom. 	Mexico declares war against the United States in 1846. The war ends two years later.	The Crimean War is fought between Russia on one side and the Ottoman Empire, Great Britain, France, and Sardinia on the other side.

Activity

The United States Constitution did not mention political parties. Parties developed as the political participation of U.S. citizens grew during the Expansion and Reform Era. Political parties helped people with similar ideas gain power.

Political parties try to persuade voters to support their candidates through advertising, fund-raising, slogans, speeches, and conventions. Conventions are meetings sponsored by political parties for their members. At conventions, members discuss issues, who will be their candidates, and campaign strategies.

Political parties hold national conventions in presidential election years. The parties hold smaller, state-level conventions in other years. At a national convention, such as the Democratic Convention or the Republican Convention, the parties vote to decide their presidential candidate. Once they are nominated, the candidates then choose a vice presidential running mate. How would you create a new political party? First, create a list of what you believe are the most important issues in the United States right now. Decide how you stand on these issues. Your stance will become the party's platform. You also need to think of a name for your party.

Pretend you have been nominated to be the party's presidential candidate. Prepare a speech about the issues you listed and your stance on them. In your speech, you need to say how you will solve the issues facing the United States if you are elected.

Quiz

1. Which U.S. president was the first son whose father was also president?
   A. James Madison
   B. Franklin Pierce
   C. John Quincy Adams

2. True or False? Millard Fillmore was the U.S. President who signed the Fugitive Slave Law.

3. Which U.S. President had the shortest term in office?
   A. William Henry Harrison
   B. Martin Van Buren
   C. John Tyler

4. True or False? The Texans won the Battle of the Alamo.

5. Who was the last member of the Whig party to serve as president?
   A. James Polk
   B. Millard Fillmore
   C. James Buchanan

6. True or False? John Quincy Adams helped create the Monroe Doctrine.

7. True or False? The Trail of Tears occurred during Andrew Jackson's presidency.

8. The United States acquired Florida under the terms of which treaty?
   A. Treaty of Paris
   B. Treaty of Ghent
   C. Adams-Onís Treaty

9. The term Manifest Destiny was used to:
   A. prevent the southern states from leaving the Union.
   B. describe expansion towards the Pacific Ocean.
   C. abolish slavery.

Answers 1. C 2. True 3. A 4. False. The Mexicans won the Battle of the Alamo. 5. B 6. True 7. False. The Trail of Tears took place during Martin Van Buren's presidency 8. C 9. B

Further Research

Books

To find out more about U.S. presidents, visit your local library. Most libraries have computers that connect to a database for researching information. If you enter a keyword, you will be provided with a list of books in the library that contain information on that topic. Non-fiction books are arranged numerically, using their call number. Fiction books are organized alphabetically by the author's last name.

Websites

The World Wide Web is also a good source of information. Reputable websites usually include government sites, educational sites, and online encyclopedias. Visit the following sites to learn more about U.S. presidents.

The official White House website offers a short history of the U.S. presidency, along with biographical sketches and portraits of all the presidents to date. **www.whitehouse.gov/history/presidents**

This website contains background information, election results, cabinet members, and notable events for each of the presidents. **www.ipl.org/div/potus**

Explore the lives and careers of every U.S. president on the PBS website.
www.pbs.org/wgbh/amex/presidents

Glossary

abolitionists: people who are opposed to slavery

amendment: a revision or change made to a law, bill, or document

annexation: adding to property; Southern politicians wanted to annex Texas, adding it to the Union

cabinet: the committee of advisors to the president, including the secretary of state and secretary of war

charter: a written grant of rights allowing a company to operate; the U.S. government gave the Second Bank of the United States a charter that expired in 1836

cholera: a disease that affects the small intestines, causing vomiting and diarrhea

delegates: members of a political party that attend the party's national convention in order to decide who will represent the party in upcoming elections

dynasty: a line of rulers

inflation: when the cost of goods rises and the value of money falls

mutiny: to rebel against people in charge

states' rights: the ability of states to govern themselves; Southerners supported states rights, whereas Northerners believed a strong federal government should have power over states

tariffs: taxes on goods imported into a country

treaty: an agreement between two sides of a conflict

vetoed: used the right to reject legislation that someone does not agree with

Whig candidate: a member of a political party that was created to oppose Andrew Jackson and his supporters

Index